INTRODUCTION

Welcome to the world of untold wealth! In a society driven by financial success and prosperity, the pursuit of wealth has become a universal aspiration. However, building substantial wealth is not merely a matter of luck or chance; it is an art that requires skill, knowledge, and strategic planning. In this era of endless possibilities, mastering the art of building untold wealth has become an essential endeavor for those who seek financial freedom and abundance. Whether you are a seasoned investor, an aspiring entrepreneur, or someone looking to enhance their financial well-being, this journey towards mastering the art of building untold wealth promises to be both enlightening and transformative. So, fasten your seatbelts as we embark on a captivating exploration of the principles, strategies, and mindset required to unlock the doors to unimaginable riches. Get ready to unleash your potential and discover the secrets that will empower you to create a life of limitless abundance.

UNDERSTANDING THE TRUE MEANING OF WEALTH

Understanding the true meaning of wealth goes beyond the conventional notion of financial abundance. While money and material possessions are often associated with wealth, true wealth encompasses a broader perspective that includes various aspects of life. Here are a few key elements to consider when exploring the true meaning of wealth:

1. Health and Well-being: True wealth involves having good physical and mental health. Without good health, all the money and possessions in the world may not bring happiness or fulfillment. Prioritizing self-care, maintaining a balanced lifestyle, and nurturing positive relationships contribute to overall well-being.

2. Relationships and Connections: Wealth can be measured by the quality of relationships and connections we have with others. Meaningful connections, supportive friendships, and loving relationships enrich our lives and provide a sense of belonging and fulfillment.

3. Personal Growth and Development: True wealth includes continuous personal growth and development. Expanding knowledge, acquiring new skills, and pursuing passions and interests contribute to a sense of purpose and fulfillment.

4. Time and Freedom: Having control over one's time and the freedom to choose how to spend it is a form of wealth. Time is a valuable resource that allows for pursuing meaningful experiences, spending time with loved ones, and engaging in activities that bring joy and fulfillment.

5. Contribution and Impact: True wealth involves making a positive impact on the world and contributing to the well-being of others. Engaging in acts of kindness, giving back to the community, and making a difference in the lives of others can bring a deep sense of fulfillment and purpose.

6. Inner Peace and Contentment: True wealth includes inner peace and contentment. It is about finding happiness and satisfaction within oneself, regardless of external circumstances. Cultivating gratitude, practicing mindfulness, and embracing a positive mindset contribute to inner wealth.

Understanding the true meaning of wealth involves recognizing that it extends beyond financial measures. It encompasses various aspects of life, including health, relationships, personal growth, time, contribution, and inner peace. By embracing a holistic perspective, we can strive for a more fulfilling and meaningful life.

DEBUNKING COMMON MISCONCEPTIONS ABOUT RICHES

Misconception 1: Riches guarantee happiness: One common misconception is that having a lot of money automatically leads to happiness. While financial stability can certainly contribute to a sense of security and comfort, studies have shown that beyond a certain income threshold, additional wealth does not significantly increase happiness. Happiness is a complex emotion influenced by various factors such as relationships, personal fulfillment, and overall well-being.

Misconception 2: Riches are solely a result of luck: While luck can play a role in financial success, it is often an oversimplification to attribute all riches to luck alone. Many wealthy individuals have achieved their wealth through hard work, perseverance, and strategic decision-making. Factors such as education, skills, entrepreneurship, and seizing opportunities also contribute to financial success.

Misconception 3: Riches are always acquired through unethical means: While there are instances of individuals acquiring wealth through unethical practices, it is incorrect to assume that all wealthy people engage in such behavior. Many individuals have built their fortunes through ethical means, such as creating innovative products or services, investing wisely, or running successful businesses. It is important to avoid generalizations and recognize that wealth can be obtained through various legitimate avenues.

Misconception 4: Riches are a measure of personal worth: Another misconception is equating financial wealth with personal worth or value. The amount of money one possesses does not define their character, intelligence, or overall worth as a human being. Personal qualities such as kindness, empathy, integrity, and personal growth are not necessarily correlated with financial status. It is crucial to recognize that everyone has unique strengths and contributions to make, regardless of their financial situation.

Misconception 5: Riches bring an end to all problems: While financial resources can help address certain challenges, they do not eliminate all problems in life. Rich individuals still face personal, health, and relationship issues like anyone else. Money cannot buy good health, genuine relationships, or inner peace. It is important to focus on holistic well-being and not solely rely on wealth to solve all life's problems.

Debunking these misconceptions helps foster a more realistic understanding of riches and encourages a broader perspective on success and happiness.

Identifying your financial goals and aspirations is an important step in creating a roadmap for your financial future. Consider the questions below to help you get started:

1. **What are Your Short-term Financial Goals?** These are goals you want to achieve within the next year or two. Examples could include building an emergency fund, paying off credit card debt, or saving for a vacation.

2. **What are Your Medium-term Financial Goals?** These are goals you want to achieve within the next 3 to 5 years. Examples could include buying a car, saving for a down payment on a house, or starting a business.

3. **What are Your Long-term Financial Goals?** These are goals you want to achieve in 10 years or more. Examples could include saving for retirement, funding your children's education, or achieving financial independence.

4. **What Lifestyle Aspirations Do You Have?** Consider the kind of lifestyle you want to lead in the future. Do you want to travel extensively, own a second home, or pursue a particular hobby or passion? These aspirations can help shape your financial goals.

5. **What Is Your Risk Tolerance?** Understanding your risk tolerance is crucial in determining your investment strategy. Are you comfortable with taking higher risks for potentially higher returns, or do you prefer a more conservative approach?

6. **What Is Your Current Financial Situation?** Assess your income, expenses, assets, and liabilities. Understanding your current financial standing will help you set realistic goals and determine the steps needed to achieve them.

7. **Are There Any Specific Milestones or Events You Want To Plan For?** Examples could include getting married, starting a family, or changing careers. These milestones may require additional financial planning.

Always remember that financial goals need to be specific, measurable, achievable, relevant, and time-bound (SMART). Once you have identified your goals and aspirations, you can start developing a financial plan to work towards them.

CULTIVATING A POSITIVE RELATIONSHIP WITH MONEY

Cultivating a positive relationship with money is essential for financial well-being and overall happiness. Here are some tips to help you develop a healthy mindset towards money:

1. Understand Your Beliefs and Attitudes: Reflect on your beliefs about money and where they come from. Identify any negative beliefs or limiting ones that may be pulling you back. Challenge these beliefs and ensure you replace them with positive and uplifting thoughts.

2. Practice Gratitude: Appreciate what you have and focus on the abundance in your life. Gratitude helps shift your mindset from scarcity to abundance, allowing you to attract more positive financial experiences.

3. Set Clear Financial Goals: Define your short-term and long-term financial goals. Having a clear vision of what you want to achieve will motivate you to make better financial decisions and take actions that align with your goals.

4. Create a Budget: Develop a budget that aligns with your goals and values. Track your income and expenses to gain a better understanding of your financial situation. A budget helps you prioritize your spending and save for the future.

5. Educate Yourself: Increase your financial literacy by reading books, attending seminars, or taking online courses. Understanding personal finance concepts, such as budgeting, investing, and debt management, empowers you to make informed decisions and take control of your financial life.

6. Practice Mindful Spending: Before making a purchase, ask yourself if it aligns with your values and goals. Avoid impulsive buying and focus on spending money on things that truly bring you joy and add value to your life.

7. Save and Invest Wisely: Develop a habit of saving money regularly. Build an emergency fund for unexpected expenses and save for future goals. Also, don't forget to invest your money wisely to grow your wealth over the long term.

8. Surround Yourself With Positive Influences: Surround yourself with people who have a healthy relationship with money. Engage in conversations about personal finance and seek advice from those who have achieved financial success.

9. Practice Self-care: Taking care of your physical and mental well-being is crucial for maintaining a positive relationship with money. Stress and anxiety can often lead to impulsive financial decisions. Give priority to self-care activities such as exercises, meditations, and spending quality time with your loved ones.

10. Give Back: Cultivate a mindset of abundance by giving back to others. Donate to causes you care about or volunteer your time. Generosity and acts of kindness create a positive cycle of abundance and gratitude.

Remember, cultivating a positive relationship with money is a journey that requires patience and consistency

WAYS TO OVERCOME LIMITING BELIEFS AND DEVELOP A GROWTH MINDSET

Overcoming limiting beliefs and developing a growth mindset are essential for personal growth and achieving success. Here are some steps you can take to work on these areas:

1. Identify Your Limiting Beliefs: Start by recognizing the beliefs that hold you back. These beliefs often manifest as negative self-talk or thoughts that undermine your confidence and abilities. Write them down and reflect on how they impact your life.

2. Challenge Your Beliefs: Once you've identified your limiting beliefs, question their validity. You need to ask yourself if there is any evidence to back them or if they are may speculations. Look for alternative perspectives and consider the possibility of a different outcome.

3. Replace With Empowering Beliefs: Replace those your limiting beliefs with more empowering ones. Choose beliefs that support your growth and potential. For example, if you believe you're not good at public speaking, replace it with the belief that you can improve your public speaking skills with practice and effort.

4. Practice Positive Self-talk: Pay attention to your inner dialogue and replace negative self-talk with positive affirmations. Stir up your spirit, recognize your progress, and focus on your strengths. This helps rewire your mindset and build self-confidence.

5. Embrace Challenges and Failures: Adopt a growth mindset by seeing challenges and failures as opportunities for learning and growth. Embrace them as stepping stones toward success rather than setbacks. View mistakes as valuable feedback and adjust your approach accordingly.

6. Set Realistic Goals: Set specific, measurable, attainable, relevant, and time-bound (SMART) goals that align with your growth mindset. Break them down into smaller, manageable steps to track your progress and celebrate achievements along the way.

7. Surround Yourself With Positive Influences: Surround yourself with people who have a growth mindset and support your personal development. Engage in communities, read books, listen to podcasts, or attend workshops that inspire and motivate you to overcome limiting beliefs.

8. Continuous Learning and Self-improvement: Cultivate a habit of continuous learning. Seek new knowledge, acquire new skills, and challenge yourself to step out of your comfort zone. Embrace lifelong learning as a way to expand your capabilities and overcome self-imposed limitations.

Remember that developing a growth mindset is an ongoing process. Be patient with yourself, be kind to yourself and celebrate your successes along the way.

HARNESSING THE POWER OF VISUALIZATION AND AFFIRMATIONS

Harnessing the power of visualization and affirmations can be a powerful tool for personal growth and achieving your goals. Here's how you can effectively utilize these techniques:

1. Set Clear Goals: Start by defining your goals and be specific about what you want to achieve. Whether it's improving your health, advancing in your career, or enhancing your relationships, having a clear vision is essential.

2. Create a Mental Image: Visualize yourself already achieving your goals. Close your eyes and imagine every detail of your desired outcome. See yourself in that situation, experiencing the emotions and sensations associated with it. The more vivid and detailed your mental image, the more powerful the visualization becomes.

3. Practice Regularly: Dedicate time each day to visualize your goals. You can do this in the morning, before bed, or during your quiet times in the day. Consistency is key to reinforce the image in your mind and align your subconscious with your conscious desires.

4. Use Positive Affirmations: Affirmations are positive statements that reinforce your beliefs and intentions. Create affirmations that reflect your goals and repeat them to yourself regularly. For example, if your goal is to improve your confidence, you can say, "I am confident, capable, and worthy of success."

5. Engage Your Senses: When visualizing, engage all your senses. Imagine how things look, sound, smell, taste, and feel. By involving your senses, you make the visualization more realistic and compelling.

6. Believe In Yourself: Cultivate a strong belief in your ability to achieve your goals. Trust that the universe is working in your favor and that you have the skills and resources to succeed. This positive mindset will enhance the effectiveness of your visualizations and affirmations.

7. Take Inspired Action: Visualization and affirmations are powerful tools, but they should be complemented by action. Take steps towards your goals, make decisions aligned with your vision, and seize opportunities that come your way. Your actions will reinforce your belief in your abilities and bring you closer to your desired outcomes.

Remember, harnessing the power of visualization and affirmations requires patience and consistency. With practice, you can reprogram your mind, overcome limiting beliefs, and manifest the life you desire.

CREATING A BUDGET AND EFFECTIVE MONEY MANAGEMENT STRATEGIES

Creating a budget and implementing effective money management strategies are essential for achieving financial stability and reaching your financial goals. Below is a step-by-step guide that can help you get started:

1. **Assess your current financial situation.** Start by assessing your income, expenses, debts and savings. This will clarify your financial obligations.

2. **Set Financial Goals:** Determine your short- and long-term financial goals. These could include saving for emergencies, paying off debts, buying a house, or planning for retirement. Setting specific and measurable goals will help you stay focused and motivated.

3. **Track Your Expenses:** Keep a record of all your expenses for a month or two. Categorize them into fixed expenses (rent, utilities, loan payments) and variable expenses (groceries, entertainment, dining out). This will help you identify areas where you can cut back and save money.

4. **Create a Budget:** Based on your income and expenses, create a monthly budget. Allocate a portion of your income towards essential expenses, savings, debt repayment, and discretionary spending. Ensure that your expenses do not exceed your income.

5. **Prioritize Savings:** Make saving a priority in your budget. Aim to save at least 10-20% of your income each month. Set up automatic transfers to a separate savings account to make it easier to save consistently.

6. **Reduce Unnecessary Expenses:** Review your variable expenses and identify areas where you can cut back. This could involve reducing dining out, entertainment expenses, or finding cheaper alternatives for certain products or services.

7. **Pay Off Debts Strategically:** If you have outstanding debts, develop a plan to pay them off systematically. Consider using the debt snowball or debt avalanche method to prioritize and pay off debts efficiently.

8. **Build an Emergency Fund:** Set aside a portion of your savings to create an emergency fund. Aim to save three to six months' worth of living expenses to cover for unforseen financial setbacks.

9. Review and Adjust Your Budget Regularly: Regularly review your budget to ensure it aligns with your financial goals and lifestyle. Make necessary adjustments to account for changes in income, expenses, and financial priorities.

10. Seek Professional Advice If Needed: If you find it challenging to manage your finances or need expert guidance, consider consulting a financial advisor who can provide personalized advice based on your specific circumstances.

effective money management requires discipline, consistency, and a willingness to make necessary adjustments.

EMBRACING FRUGALITY AND THE IMPORTANCE OF SAVING

Frugality and saving money are essential habits that can lead to financial stability and long-term success. Here are some key points to embrace frugality and understand the importance of saving:

1. Budgeting: Create a monthly budget to track your income and expenses. This will help you identify areas where you can cut back and save more.

2. Differentiate Between Needs and Wants: Prioritize your spending by distinguishing between essential needs and discretionary wants. Focus on fulfilling your needs first and then allocate funds for wants if there is room in your budget.

3. Comparison Shopping: Before making a purchase, compare prices from different sellers or brands. Look for discounts, sales, or alternative options to get the best value for your money.

4. Avoid Impulse Buying: Take time to consider your purchases. Impulse buying often leads to unnecessary expenses. Wait for a day or two before making non-essential purchases to ensure you genuinely need or want the item.

5. Cut Back On Unnecessary Expenses: Identify areas where you can reduce costs. This could include eating out less frequently, canceling unused subscriptions, or finding cheaper alternatives for everyday items.

6. Save On Utilities: Be mindful of your energy and water consumption. Turn off lights when not in use, unplug electronics, and consider energy-efficient appliances. Additionally, fix any leaks or insulate your home to save on water and heating bills.

7. Cook at Home: Eating out can be expensive. Embrace cooking at home and meal planning to save money on groceries and reduce food waste.

8. Embrace Second-hand Shopping: Consider buying used items instead of always opting for brand new ones. Thrift stores, online marketplaces, and garage sales can offer great deals on various items.

9. Automate Savings: Set up automatic transfers from your checking account to a savings account each month. This way, you can continue to save money without being tempted to spend it elsewhere.

10. Set Financial Goals: Define short-term and long-term financial goals. Whether it's building an emergency fund, saving for a down payment, or planning for retirement, having clear goals will motivate you to save more.

Remember, frugality doesn't mean depriving yourself of everything enjoyable. It's about making conscious choices to prioritize your financial well-being and find a balance between saving and spending wisely.

NAVIGATING THE WORLD OF DEBT INTELLIGENTLY

Navigating the world of debt intelligently is crucial for maintaining financial stability and achieving long-term financial goals. Here are some tips to help you manage your debt wisely:

1. Understand Your Debt: Start by gathering all the necessary information about your debts, including the outstanding balances, interest rates, and repayment terms. This will give you a clear picture of your financial obligations.

2. Create a Budget: Create a realistic budget that outlines your income, expenses, and debt repayments. Allocate a portion of your income towards debt repayment while ensuring you have enough for essential expenses and savings.

3. Prioritize High-interest Debt: If you have multiple debts, prioritize paying off those with the highest interest rates first. This approach minimizes the amount of interest you'll pay over time and helps you become debt-free faster.

4. Explore Debt Consolidation: If you have multiple debts with varying interest rates,consider consolidating them into a single loan with a lower interest rate. Debt consolidation can simplify your payments and potentially save you money on interest.

5. Negotiate With Creditors: If you're struggling to make your debt payments, reach out to your creditors and explain your situation. They may be willing to negotiate a lower interest rate, a temporary payment plan, or even a debt settlement.

6. Avoid Taking On New Debt: While repaying your existing debt, try to avoid taking on additional debt. Minimize the use of credit cards and focus on living within your means. This will prevent your debt from spiraling out of control.

7. Seek Professional Advice: If you're overwhelmed or unsure about managing your debt, consider seeking advice from a financial advisor or credit counseling agency. They can give you personalized advice and help you come up with a debt repayment plan.

8. Stay Organized: Keep track of your debt payments, due dates, and any correspondence with creditors. Staying organized will help you avoid late payments, penalties, and unnecessary stress.

 managing debt intelligently requires discipline, patience, and a commitment to financial well-being. By implementing these strategies and making responsible financial choices, you can regain control of your debt and work towards a debt-free future.

LEVERAGING YOUR SKILLS AND FINDING YOUR NICHE

Leveraging your skills and finding your niche is essential for personal and professional growth. Here are some steps to help you identify your skills and discover your niche:

1. **Self-assessment:** Assessing your interests, skills, and strengths is a good start. Think about what you like, what you're good at, and what comes to your mind naturally. Consider your past experiences, hobbies, and any specialized knowledge you possess.

2. **Identify Market Demands:** Research the market to identify areas where there is a demand for specific skills or expertise. Look for industries or sectors that align with your interests and have growth potential. This will help you narrow down your options and focus on areas where your skills can be valuable.

3. **Explore Different Opportunities:** Experiment with different roles, projects, or industries to gain exposure and discover what resonates with you. This could involve taking on freelance work, volunteering, or pursuing internships. By exploring various opportunities, you can gain insights into different fields and identify where your skills are most valued.

4. **Seek Feedback:** Reach out to mentors, colleagues, or professionals in your desired field and seek their feedback on your skills and potential niche. Their insights can provide valuable perspectives and help you identify areas where you can excel.

5. **Continuous Learning:** Invest in continuous learning and skill development. Stay updated with industry trends, attend workshops or seminars, and pursue relevant certifications or courses. This will enhance your skill set and make you more competitive in your chosen niche.

6. **Test and Refine:** Once you have identified a potential niche, test it out. Start by taking on small projects or clients within that niche to gauge your interest and assess your performance. Use this experience to refine your skills and build a portfolio that showcases your expertise.

7. **Network and Collaborate:** Build a strong professional network within your niche. Make out time to attend industry events, join relevant online communities, and connect with people of like-mind. Collaborating with others in your niche can open up new opportunities and help you gain visibility.

8. Adapt and Evolve: As you progress in your niche, be open to adapting and evolving. Stay agile and embrace new technologies, trends, and opportunities that arise. This will ensure that you remain relevant and continue to grow within your chosen niche.

finding your niche takes time and exploration. Be patient and be willing to consistently take calculated risks. By leveraging your skills and focusing on a niche that aligns with your passion and market demand, you can position yourself for success and fulfillment in your personal and professional life.

EXPLORING DIFFERENT TYPES OF INCOME STREAMS

Exploring different types of income streams can provide financial stability and flexibility. Here are the three main types of income streams to consider: active, passive, and residual.

1. Active Income: Active income is earned through direct participation or exchange of time and effort. It typically involves trading your skills, knowledge, or labor for money. Examples include salaries, wages, commissions, or income from self-employment. Active income requires ongoing work and is directly proportional to the time and effort you invest.

2. Passive Income: Passive income is earned with minimal effort or ongoing involvement once the initial setup is done. It often involves leveraging assets, investments, or systems to generate income. Examples include rental income, dividends from stocks, interest from savings accounts, or royalties from intellectual property. Passive income allows you to earn money even when you're not actively working.

3. Residual Income: Residual income is earned through ongoing work or effort that you have already completed. It is typically associated with businesses or ventures where you continue to receive income from past work. Examples include royalties from books, music, or software, network marketing commissions, or affiliate marketing. Residual income allows you to earn money repeatedly from a single effort.

To Explore Different Income Streams:

1. Assess Your Skills and Interests: Identify your strengths, talents, and areas of expertise. This will help you determine which income streams align with your abilities and passions.

2. Research Opportunities: Explore different income streams within your chosen category. For active income, consider job opportunities, freelance work, or starting your own business. For passive income, research investment options, real estate, or online businesses. For residual income, explore opportunities in creative fields, network marketing, or affiliate marketing.

3. Diversify Your Income: Consider diversifying your income streams to reduce risk and increase stability. Having multiple sources of income can provide a safety net and protect you from relying solely on one stream.

4. Invest in Education and Skill Development: Continuously invest in learning and developing new skills. This will enhance your ability to generate income and open up new opportunities in different income streams.

5. Take Calculated Risks: Some income streams may require initial investments or taking calculated risks. Evaluate the potential returns, assess the risks involved, and make informed decisions.

6. Monitor and Adapt: Regularly monitor your income streams and assess their performance. Be open to adapting and adjusting your strategies based on market trends, changes in demand, or personal circumstances.

Remember, building multiple income streams takes time, effort, and perseverance. It's important to find a balance between active, passive, and residual income streams that align with your goals and lifestyle.

STRATEGIES FOR STARTING A SIDE BUSINESS OR INVESTING IN PROFITABLE VENTURES

Starting a side business or investing in profitable ventures can be an exciting and rewarding endeavor. Here are some strategies to consider:

1. Identify Your Passion and Skills: Firstly, identify your interests, then your skills. Look for opportunities that align with your expertise and passion. Doing this will increase the chances of your success and make the journey interesting.

2. Conduct Market Research: Before starting a side business or investing, conduct thorough market research. Identify target customers, analyze competitors, and assess market demand. This will help you understand the viability and potential profitability of your venture.

3. Develop a Business Plan: Create a comprehensive business plan that outlines your goals, strategies, target market, financial projections, and marketing approach. A well-structured plan acts as a roadmap and will help you stay focused on your goals.

4. Start Small and Test The Waters: Consider starting small to minimize risks and gain valuable experience. Launch a pilot project or test your product/service in a limited market. This will allow you to gather feedback, make necessary adjustments, and validate your business idea before scaling up.

5. Leverage Your Network: Utilize your personal and professional network to gain support, seek advice, and explore potential partnerships. Networking can provide valuable insights, mentorship, and access to resources that can accelerate your business growth.

6. Seek Professional Advice: Consult with professionals such as accountants, lawyers, or business advisors to ensure compliance with legal and financial requirements. They can guide you through the process, help you make informed decisions, and mitigate potential risks.

7. Diversify Your Investments: If you're considering investing in profitable ventures, diversify your portfolio to spread the risk. Invest in different industries, asset classes, or geographical regions. This will help protect your investments from market fluctuations and increase the likelihood of overall profitability.

8. Stay Informed and Educated: Continuously educate yourself about the industry trends, market dynamics, and investment strategies. Attend workshops, seminars, or webinars, read books, and follow reputable sources of information. Staying informed will enable you to make informed decisions and adapt to changing market conditions.

9. Monitor and Evaluate: Regularly monitor the performance of your side business or investments. Track key metrics, analyze financial statements, and assess the effectiveness of your strategies. This allows you to identify areas that need improvement and make the necessary changes to maximize profitability.

10. Be Patient and Persistent: Building a successful side business or investment portfolio takes time and effort. Be patient, stay committed, and learn from failures.

UNDERSTANDING DIFFERENT INVESTMENT VEHICLES

Understanding different investment vehicles is crucial when considering where to allocate your funds. Here is an overview of some common investment options to consider:

1. **Stocks:** Stocks represent ownership in a company. When you buy shares of a company's stock, you become a partial owner and can benefit from capital appreciation and dividends. Stocks can be purchased through brokerage accounts, and their value fluctuates based on market conditions and the company's performance.

2. **Real Estate:** Real estate investments involve purchasing properties such as residential homes, commercial buildings, or land. Real estate can generate income through rental payments or appreciation in property value. It can provide both short-term cash flow and long-term wealth accumulation.

3. **Mutual Funds:** Mutual funds pool money from multiple investors to invest in a diversified portfolio of stocks, bonds, or other assets. They are managed by professional fund managers who make investment decisions on behalf of the investors. Mutual funds offer diversification, liquidity, and professional management, making them suitable for investors seeking a hands-off approach.

4. **Exchange-Traded Funds (ETFs):** ETFs are similar to mutual funds, but they trade on stock exchanges like individual stocks. Provides diversification by following an index, sector, or asset class. ETFs offer more flexibility, transparency, and lower expense ratios than mutual funds.

5. **Bonds:** Bonds are debt instruments issued by governments, municipalities, or corporations to raise capital. When you purchase a bond, you are essentially lending money to the issuer in exchange for periodic interest payments and repayment of the principal at maturity. Bonds are considered a less risky investment than stocks, but they generally offer lower returns.

6. **Commodities:** Commodities include physical goods like gold, oil, natural gas, agricultural products, etc. Investors can gain exposure to commodities through futures contracts, exchange-traded funds (ETFs), or commodity-specific mutual funds. Commodities can act as a hedge against inflation and provide diversification benefits.

7. **Options and Derivatives:** Options and derivatives are financial instruments derived from underlying assets such as stocks, bonds, or commodities. They provide investors with the right,

but not the obligation, to buy or sell the underlying asset at a predetermined price within a specified time frame. Options and derivatives can be complex and carry higher risks, requiring a good understanding of the market.

It's important to note that each investment vehicle carries its own risks, rewards, and considerations. It's advisable to conduct thorough research, seek professional advice, and align your investment choices with your financial goals, risk tolerance, and time horizon.

RISK MANAGEMENT AND DIVERSIFICATION

Risk management and diversification are two important concepts in the world of finance and investing.

- **Risk Management** refers to the process of identifying, assessing, and mitigating potential risks that may impact the achievement of financial goals. It involves understanding the various types of risks, such as market risk, credit risk, operational risk, and liquidity risk, and implementing strategies to minimize their impact. This can be done through diversification, which is the practice of spreading investments across different asset classes, sectors, regions, or even currencies. By diversifying, investors can reduce their exposure to any single investment or asset, thereby potentially reducing the overall risk in their portfolio.

- **Diversification** is based on the principle that different assets or investments may perform differently under different market conditions. By holding a mix of investments, including stocks, bonds, real estate, and commodities, for example, an investor can potentially benefit from the positive performance of one asset class while mitigating the negative impact of another. Diversification does not guarantee profits or protect against losses, but it can help to manage risk and potentially enhance long-term returns.

In all, risk management and diversification are essential tools for investors to protect their portfolios from potential risks and increase the likelihood of achieving their financial objectives. These are important elements of a well-thought-out investment strategy. Below is an overview of these concepts:

1. **Risk Management:** Risk management involves identifying, assessing, and mitigating potential risks associated with investments. Here are some key principles:

   a. **Risk Assessment:** Evaluate the risk-return trade-off of each investment. Higher-risk investments may offer higher potential returns but also carry greater volatility and potential losses.

b. Asset Allocation: Diversify your portfolio across different asset classes (e.g., stocks, bonds, real estate) to reduce the impact of any single investment's performance on your overall portfolio.

c. Risk Tolerance: Understand your risk tolerance, which is your ability and willingness to withstand potential losses. It helps determine the appropriate level of risk in your portfolio.

d. Stop-loss Orders: Consider using stop-loss orders to automatically sell an investment if it reaches a predetermined price, limiting potential losses.

e. Regular Monitoring: Continuously monitor your investments to stay informed about market conditions, company performance, and any changes that may affect your portfolio.

2. **Diversification:** Diversification involves spreading your investments across different asset classes, industries, geographic regions, and investment vehicles. Here's why it's important:

a. Risk Reduction: Diversification helps reduce the impact of a single investment's poor performance on your overall portfolio. If one investment underperforms, others may offset the losses.

b. Potential Returns: While diversification cannot eliminate all risks, it can enhance the potential for consistent returns by capturing gains from different investments.

c. Asset Class Diversification: Allocate your investments across various asset classes (e.g., stocks, bonds, real estate) to balance risk and return. Different asset classes tend to perform differently under varying market conditions.

d. Geographic Diversification: Invest in different regions or countries to reduce exposure to any single economy or political environment.

e. Sector Diversification: Spread investments across different sectors (e.g., technology, healthcare, energy) to avoid concentration risk in a specific industry.

f. Investment Vehicle Diversification: Consider diversifying across various investment vehicles, such as stocks, bonds, mutual funds, and ETFs, to access different risk profiles and potential returns.

Remember, diversification does not guarantee profits or protect against losses, but it can help manage risk and increase the likelihood of achieving long-term investment goals. Regularly review and rebalance your portfolio to maintain diversification as market conditions and your financial objectives change.

NAVIGATING THE VOLATILE NATURE OF FINANCIAL MARKETS

Navigating the volatile nature of financial markets can be challenging, but there are several strategies that can help you manage and mitigate risks. Here are a few suggestions:

1. Diversify Your Portfolio: By spreading your investments across different asset classes, industries, and geographical regions, you can reduce the impact of market volatility on your overall portfolio. Diversification helps to minimize losses in one area by potentially gaining in another.

2. Stay Informed: Keep yourself updated on the latest news and trends in the financial markets. Understanding the factors that drive market movements, such as economic indicators, geopolitical events, and industry-specific news, can help you make informed investment decisions.

3. Have a Long-term Perspective: Financial markets can experience short-term fluctuations, but taking a long-term approach can help you ride out volatility and benefit from potential growth over time. Stay focused on your investment goals and stick to your strategy.

4. Set Realistic Expectations: It's important to have realistic expectations about the returns you can achieve in the financial markets. Avoid making impulsive decisions based on short-term market movements, as this can lead to costly mistakes.

5. Consider Risk Management Tools: Utilize risk management tools such as stop-loss orders and trailing stops to protect your investments. These tools can automatically sell your positions if they reach a predetermined price, limiting potential losses.

6. Seek Professional Advice: Consider working with a financial advisor who can provide personalized guidance based on your financial goals, risk tolerance, and market conditions. A professional can help you navigate through market volatility and make informed decisions.

while it's impossible to predict or control market movements, you can take steps to manage risk and make informed investment decisions.

UNLEASHING YOUR CREATIVE POTENTIAL AND IDENTIFYING ENTREPRENEURIAL OPPORTUNITIES

Unleashing your creative potential and identifying entrepreneurial opportunities can be an exciting and fulfilling journey. The following steps can help you in this process:

1. **Embrace Curiosity and Open-mindedness:** Cultivate a mindset that is open to new ideas, perspectives, and possibilities. Be curious about the world around you and seek out diverse experiences and knowledge.

2. **Explore Your Passions and Interests:** Reflect on what truly excites and motivates you. Identify your passions and interests, as they often serve as a foundation for creative thinking and entrepreneurial endeavors.

3. **Develop Your Creative Skills:** Creativity is a skill that can be nurtured and developed. Engage in activities that stimulate your imagination, such as brainstorming, mind mapping, or engaging in artistic pursuits. Practice thinking outside the box and challenging conventional wisdom.

4. **Stay Informed and Observe Trends:** Keep yourself updated on the latest trends, technologies, and market developments. Read books, attend conferences, follow industry influencers, and engage in discussions to gain insights into emerging opportunities.

5. **Identify Problems and Pain Points:** Look for problems or challenges that people face in their daily lives. These can be opportunities for entrepreneurial ventures. Consider how you can provide innovative solutions or improve existing products/services.

6. **Conduct Market Research:** Once you have identified a potential opportunity, conduct thorough market research. Understand your target audience, competition, market size, and potential demand. This will help you validate your idea and refine your approach.

7. **Network and Collaborate:** Build a strong network of like-minded individuals, entrepreneurs, and mentors. Attend networking events, join entrepreneurial communities, and seek collaborations. Surrounding yourself with supportive and knowledgeable individuals can provide valuable guidance and opportunities.

8. Develop a Business Plan: Create a comprehensive business plan that outlines your vision, goals, target market, marketing strategies, financial projections, and implementation timeline. This plan will act like a roadmap for your entrepreneurial journey.

9. Take Calculated Risks: Entrepreneurship involves taking risks, but it's important to assess and manage them wisely. Evaluate the potential rewards and risks associated with each opportunity and make informed decisions.

10. Iterate and Adapt: Entrepreneurship is a dynamic process. Be prepared to iterate, adapt, and pivot as you gain insights and feedback from the market. See failures as learning opportunities and use them to improve your approach.

Remember, unleashing your creative potential and identifying entrepreneurial opportunities requires dedication, perseverance, and a willingness to step out of your comfort zone. Stay focused, believe in yourself,

TIPS FOR STARTING AND SCALING A SUCCESSFUL BUSINESS

Starting and scaling a successful business requires careful planning, strategic decision-making, and consistent effort. Below are some tips to consider, these will help you along the way:

1. Identify a Viable Business Idea: Start by identifying a problem or need in the market that your business can address. Conduct market research to validate your idea and make sure there is a high demand for your product or service.

2. Develop a Comprehensive Business Plan: A well-thought-out business plan serves as a roadmap for your business. It should include your mission, target market, competitive analysis, marketing strategy, financial projections, and operational details.

3. Build a Strong Team: Surround yourself with talented people who share your vision and complement your skills. Hire passionate, skilled employees who fit your company culture. Remember, your team is crucial to your business's success.

4. Secure Adequate Funding: Determine the financial requirements of your business and explore various funding options such as personal savings, loans, grants, or seeking investors. Make sure you have enough capital to cover initial expenses and support your business in its early stages.

5. Focus on Customer Satisfaction: Prioritize delivering exceptional customer experiences. Understand your customers' needs, provide high-quality products or services, and build strong relationships. Happy customers are more likely to become repeat customers and refer others to your business.

6. Embrace Innovation and Adaptability: Stay updated with industry trends and technological advancements. Stay open to change and adjust your business strategies accordingly. Innovation can help you stay ahead of the competition and meet evolving customer demands.

7. Implement Effective Marketing Strategies: Develop a strong brand identity and create a marketing plan to reach your target audience. Utilize various marketing channels such as social media, content marketing, SEO, and paid advertising to promote your business and attract customers.

8. Monitor and Analyze Key Metrics: Regularly track and analyze key performance indicators (KPIs) to evaluate the success of your business. This includes financial metrics, customer acquisition costs, conversion rates, and customer satisfaction. Make informed decisions using this data so as to optimize your business operations.

9. Foster a Positive Company Culture: Cultivate a positive work environment that encourages collaboration, creativity, and employee growth. A strong company culture attracts and retains top talent, boosts productivity, and enhances overall business performance.

10. Seek Mentorship and Continuous Learning: Surround yourself with experienced entrepreneurs and seek their guidance. Join industry associations, attend workshops, and invest in your own personal and professional development.

BUILDING A ROBUST PROFESSIONAL NETWORK

Building a robust professional network is essential for career growth and success. Here are some tips to help you strengthen your network:

1. Identify Your Goals: Determine what you want to achieve through your network. Whether it's finding a new job, gaining industry insights, or expanding your knowledge, having clear goals will guide your networking efforts.

2. Attend Industry Events: Attend conferences, seminars, and networking events related to your field. These provide opportunities to meet like-minded professionals, exchange ideas, and build connections.

3. Leverage Social Media: Utilize platforms like LinkedIn to connect with professionals in your industry. Join relevant groups, participate in discussions, and share insightful content to establish yourself as a thought leader.

4. Seek Mentorship: Find experienced professionals who can guide you in your career journey. Mentors can provide valuable advice, support, and introductions to their own networks.

5. Offer Help and Support: Be willing to assist others in your network. Share your knowledge, refer job opportunities, or offer support when needed. Building relationships that is mutually beneficial is the key to having a strong network.

6. Attend Informational Interviews: Request meetings with professionals you admire or who are in positions you aspire to. Use these interviews to gain insights, ask for advice, and expand your network.

7. Stay in Touch: Regularly reach out to your contacts to maintain the relationship. Congratulate them on their achievements, share relevant articles or resources, and offer your assistance whenever possible.

Remember, building a robust professional network takes time and effort. Be genuine, authentic, and proactive in your networking endeavors.

UNDERSTANDING THE IMPORTANCE OF SOCIAL RESPONSIBILITY AND GIVING

Social responsibility and giving back to the community are not only morally important but also beneficial for businesses in several ways. Below is why understanding their importance is crucial:

1. Enhancing Brand Reputation: Engaging in social responsibility initiatives and giving back to the community can significantly enhance your brand's reputation. When customers see that your business is actively involved in making a positive impact, they are more likely to trust and support your brand.

2. Building Customer Loyalty: Consumers are increasingly conscious of the social and environmental impact of businesses. By aligning your company with causes that resonate with your target audience, you can build strong emotional connections and foster customer loyalty. Customers are more likely to choose brands that demonstrate a commitment to social responsibility.

3. Attracting and Retaining Top Talent: Employees, particularly millennials and Gen Z, are increasingly seeking purpose-driven work environments. By incorporating social responsibility into your business practices, you can attract and retain top talent who are passionate about making a difference. This can lead to higher employee satisfaction, productivity, and lower turnover rates.

4. Strengthening Community Relationships: Giving back to the community helps build strong relationships with local stakeholders, including customers, suppliers, and government entities. This can lead to increased support, collaboration, and opportunities for your business.

5. Mitigating Risks and Improving Sustainability: Engaging in social responsibility initiatives can help mitigate risks associated with negative environmental or social impacts. By adopting sustainable practices, reducing waste, and supporting ethical sourcing, you can contribute to a healthier planet and a more sustainable future.

6. Creating a Positive Work Culture: Encouraging employees to participate in volunteer activities or charitable initiatives can foster a positive work culture. It promotes teamwork, empathy, and a sense of purpose among employees, leading to increased job satisfaction and overall well-being.

7. Contributing to Social Change: Businesses have the power to drive positive social change. By supporting causes that align with your values and mission, you can contribute to solving societal issues and making a meaningful impact on the lives of others.When incorporating social responsibility and giving back into your business strategy, it's important to choose causes that align with your values and have a genuine impact. Consider partnering with local nonprofits, organizing volunteer activities, or donating a portion of your profits to charitable organizations. Remember, small actions can make a big difference in creating a better world.

STRATEGIES FOR CREATING A LEGACY THROUGH PHILANTHROPIC ENDEAVORS

Creating a legacy through philanthropic endeavors is a noble pursuit that can have a lasting impact on society. Here are some strategies to consider:

1. Define Your Values and Mission: Start by identifying the causes and issues that resonate with you personally. Reflect on your values and passions to determine the areas where you want to make a difference. This will help you establish a clear mission for your philanthropic endeavors.

2. Research and Identify Effective Organizations: Conduct thorough research to identify reputable and effective organizations working in your chosen cause areas. Look for organizations with a proven track record, transparent financials, and measurable impact. Consider partnering with established nonprofits or creating your own foundation.

3. Develop a Strategic Giving Plan: Outline a strategic giving plan that aligns with your mission and goals. Determine the amount of funds you are willing to allocate, the frequency of giving, and the specific projects or initiatives you want to support. This plan will provide structure and direction to your philanthropic efforts.

4. Collaborate and Leverage Partnerships: Seek opportunities to collaborate with other philanthropists, foundations, and corporations. By pooling resources and expertise, you can amplify your impact and tackle complex social issues more effectively. Partnerships can also provide access to networks and knowledge that can enhance your philanthropic efforts.

5. Engage in Hands-on Involvement: Consider getting actively involved in the causes you support. Attend events, volunteer your time, and engage with the communities you aim to serve. This hands-on involvement will deepen your understanding of the issues and enable you to make more informed decisions about your philanthropic investments.

6. Measure and Evaluate Impact: Establish metrics and evaluation mechanisms to measure the impact of your philanthropic endeavors. Regularly assess the effectiveness of the projects or initiatives you support and make adjustments as needed. This will ensure that your resources are being utilized optimally and that you are making a meaningful difference.

7. Inspire and Involve Future Generations: Consider involving your family and future generations in your philanthropic efforts. Instill the values of giving back and create opportunities for them to actively participate in charitable activities. This will help ensure the continuity of your legacy and inspire a culture of philanthropy within your family. Creating a lasting legacy through philanthropy requires a long-term commitment, strategic thinking, and a genuine desire to make a positive impact.

BALANCING PERSONAL WEALTH WITH MAKING A POSITIVE IMPACT ON SOCIETY

Balancing personal wealth with making a positive impact on society is a complex and important consideration. Here are a few suggestions to help you navigate this balance:

1. Define Your Values: Start by identifying your personal values and what matters most to you. This will serve as a guiding principle when making decisions about wealth and impact. Consider the causes or issues you are passionate about and how you can contribute to them.

2. Align Your Financial Goals With Impact: Look for opportunities to align your financial goals with making a positive impact. This could involve investing in socially responsible companies, supporting sustainable businesses, or donating a portion of your wealth to charitable organizations. By integrating impact into your financial decisions, you can create a win-win situation.

3. Practice Conscious Consumption: Be mindful of your spending habits and the impact they have on society. Consider supporting businesses that give priority to ethical practices, fair trade, as well as sustainability. By making conscious choices, you can use your purchasing power to support positive change.

4. Volunteer and Donate: In addition to financial contributions, consider volunteering your time and skills to organizations that align with your values. This can be a meaningful way to make a positive impact while balancing personal wealth. Additionally, donating to causes you care about can help support initiatives that create social change.

5. Collaborate and Advocate: Engage with others who share your values and work together to create a larger impact. Collaborate with like-minded individuals, organizations, or communities to amplify your efforts. Additionally, use your voice to advocate for policies and practices that promote social and environmental well-being.

Remember, finding the right balance between personal wealth and making a positive impact is a personal journey. It may require ongoing reflection, adaptation, and learning. By integrating these principles into your life, you can strive for a harmonious balance that benefits both yourself and society.

CONCLUSION

Mastering the Art of Building Untold Wealth," we have covered a wide range of topics essential to achieving financial prosperity. By adopting the principles shared within this book, you can lay a strong foundation, create financial security, and build an abundant future. Remember, true wealth extends beyond material possessions; it encompasses a sense of fulfillment, freedom, and the ability to make a positive difference in the lives of others. Start your journey to unlimited possibilities today!